THE OFFICIAL
WEST HAM UNITED
ANNUAL 2007

Written by Colin Benson

A Grange Publication

ISBN 1 905426 25 9

£6.99

CONTENTS

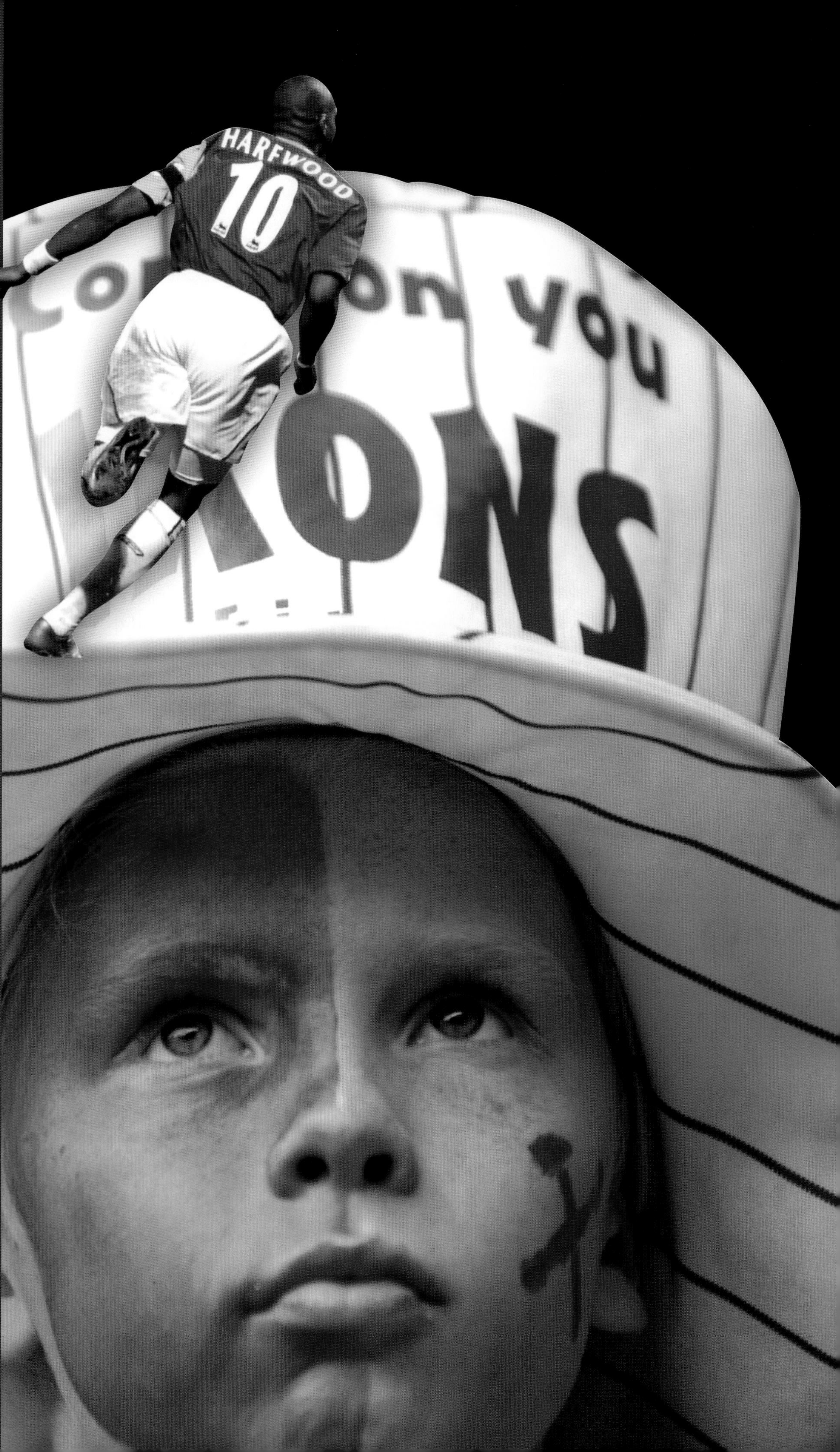
HAREWOOD
10
on you

WELCOME

TO THE OFFICIAL HAMMERS ANNUAL 2007

No Christmas would be the same without a touch of Hammers magic and for all young West Ham United fans, far and wide, the Official Club Annual brings you closer to the stars of today.

Who is the wing wizard? Who is the oldest player in the Premiership? Who is a gadget freak? Who played with Paul Konchesky and John Terry as a schoolboy? All will be revealed with many other secrets of the stars.

Following the thrills of last season we have the added excitement of European competition in the UEFA Cup this year and with Alan Pardew adding to the squad that finished last term so gloriously, in ninth place in the Barclays Premier League, this is becoming one of the most electrifying periods in the Club's history.

The big names are here and there is much, much more too. Fact files and reflections on historical moments that have made West Ham United what it is today, one of the great institutions of English football. There's a chance to take on your family and friends with quizzes and puzzles. Get Dad involved and see if you can beat him.

You can thrill again to last season's glorious FA Cup run that culminated in one of the best ever finals and look forward to the coming competition with Hayden Mullins.

All the stars are here for you to enjoy in a package embellished with glorious photography.

There is something for everyone in the Hammers Annual 2007 we hope you enjoy it.

PARDS IS A TOP BOSS

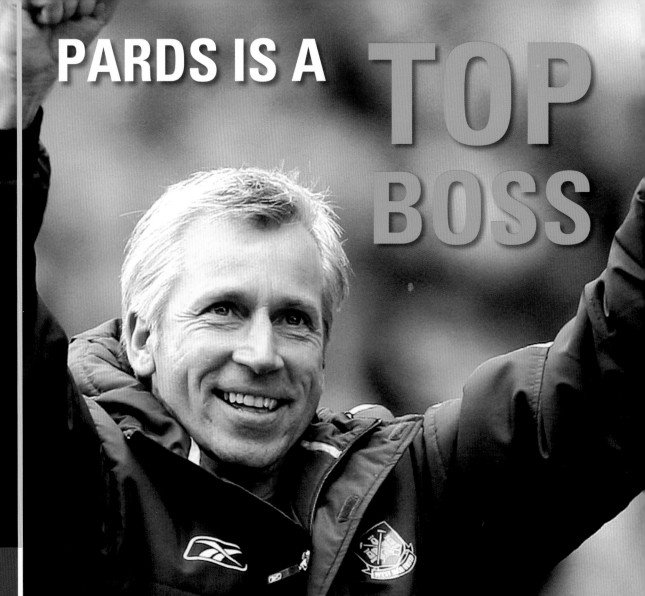

West Ham United has a proud tradition of loyalty that dates back to 1902 when the flamboyant Syd King was appointed the Club's first manager. In October 2003 Alan Pardew became only the 10th occupant of the managerial chair and last season he proved himself more than capable of one day joining the illustrious names of Ron Greenwood and John Lyall in the Hammers hall of fame.

A measure of just how quickly Pards was able to turn round the wrath of some disenchanted fans and media uncertainty as to his suitability to be the Hammers' boss into positive acclaim was emphasised last April when following the announcement of the departure of Sven Goran Eriksson his name was being touted in the media as a possible replacement as England manager.

Pards, is a very ambitious professional and no doubt he would love to follow in the footsteps of Ron Greenwood from Upton Park to Soho Square one day. But first he has a mission to not just establish West Ham United as a Premiership team but to mould them into a side that is capable of challenging for the major prizes on a regular basis.

He says: "One thing I know about West Ham, is that expectations can rise very quickly. That's why, if I'm being candid, I'm a bit cautious with the press about the Champions League and UEFA Cup. I've seen what the pressure can do to people here – the players more than myself."

Nonetheless last season's success in establishing a top 10 finish in the Barclays Premiership and entertaining the world in what was hailed by some as the greatest FA Cup Final ever he has done himself and the Club proud.

Guiding a young team through the choppy waters of the Premiership was never going to be easy yet right from the off Pards adopted a positive attitude and delivered a team that not only achieved results but did it in style – playing football the traditional Hammers way.

Pards is very mindful of the Club's history but wants his team to mirror his own strength of character and he says: "My vision is of fast football. I want the team to play with exciting pace and power, itching to come out of the stalls and being able to control the game."

The fact that the Hammers confounded the sceptics who tipped them as relegation candidates by finishing ninth in the final table and qualify for a place in the UEFA Cup through the FA Cup did not go unnoticed abroad.

France's most respected sports daily paper *L'Equipe* hailed the West Ham boss as the brightest young English manager in the Barclays Premiership.

The art of good management is not just getting the tactical side of the game right but knowing your players, their strengths and weaknesses, their moods and fluctuations and in this respect Pardew is a great psychologist.

He has used paintballing and trips to places like the golf complex at La Manga in Spain, where they played games based on quiz shows from the 1980s, to foster team spirit.

It took time to achieve but Pards got there in the end and the bonding was there for all to see in the FA Cup semi-final and final in particular – games which illustrated fully the character and togetherness of Alan Pardew's Hammers team.

He says: "Where I want to be is managing competitively against Mourinho, Benitez, Wenger and Ferguson. We're not at that level but we'll try to get there."

Last season Pards took giant strides in the right direction.

DANNY IS A TOP HAMMER

THERE was no doubt from the day that Danny Gabbidon made his Hammers debut in the opening game of last season, at home to Blackburn Rovers, that he was going to make an impact on the Premiership.

At the age of 26 the Welsh international was making his bow in the Premiership yet seemed perfectly at ease and in control up against some of the greatest strikers in the world as he settled in to become the mainstay of the defence striking up a great central defensive partnership alongside Anton Ferdinand.

Danny started his career as a youngster with West Bromwich Albion, but found himself out of favour when Gary Megson took charge at the Hawthorns and, in August 2000, he moved onto Cardiff City where he played for five years.

The Welsh star reflects: "I enjoyed my time at West Brom, but when Gary Megson arrived he didn't really fancy me as a player. I moved on and that's probably the best thing that could have happened to me at the time because I was given my chance to prove myself at Cardiff and that led to my move to West Ham."

Indeed, he won more than just admiration while playing for the Bluebirds where he developed his elegant interpretation of the role of a central-defender establishing himself as the rock at the heart of the Cardiff City defence upon which most opposition attacks floundered. At the end of the 2003-04 season at Ninian Park, in which he forged an excellent partnership with James Collins, Danny's contribution was recognised by his fellow professionals who voted him into the PFA First Division team of the season.

A quiet reserved person off the field, Danny has a great sense of humour and humility and was genuinely overwhelmed when he was named the Club's Hammer of the Year for 2006.

He gasped: "Every game was massive for me and to finish my first season at West Ham playing in the Cup Final at the Millennium Stadium against Liverpool and being chosen as the Hammer of the Year was just beyond my wildest dreams.

"It has all been very exciting and this season we have also had the bonus of competing in Europe as well in the UEFA Cup."

It really will be a busy season for Danny who besides playing his part in what he hopes will be the greatest season ever for West Ham United, is also fully committed, along with team-mate James Collins, to helping Wales qualify for the European Championship Finals in 2008.

Danny, who has pace, reads the game perfectly, and allies physical strength to a fine footballing brain, is now a regular in the Welsh team and rooms with his best pal, Rob Earnshaw (now with Norwich City), when on international duty.

There is no doubt that his calm collected approach to the game was a key component in last season's successful campaign with the Hammers and it was a fitting tribute that he should become the first central-defender to be rewarded with the ultimate Club tribute since Rio Ferdinand was crowned Hammer of the Year in 1998.

PAST HAMMERS OF THE YEAR

Year	Winner	Runner-up
1957–58	Andy Malcolm	-
1958–59	Ken Brown	-
1959–60	Malcolm Musgrove	-
1960–61	Bobby Moore	-
1961–62	Lawrie Leslie	John Dick
1962–63	Bobby Moore	Jim Standen
1963–64	Johnny Byrne	Bobby Moore
1964–65	Martin Peters	-
1965–66	Geoff Hurst	Martin Peters
1966–67	Geoff Hurst	Bobby Moore
1967–68	Bobby Moore	Trevor Brooking
1968–69	Geoff Hurst	Billy Bonds
1969–70	Bobby Moore	Billy Bonds
1970–71	Billy Bonds	Bobby Moore
1971–72	Trevor Brooking	Bobby Ferguson
1972–73	Bryan Robson	Trevor Brooking
1973–74	Billy Bonds	Mervyn Day
1974–75	Billy Bonds	Mervyn Day
1975–76	Trevor Brooking	Graham Paddon
1976–77	Trevor Brooking	Alan Devonshire
1977–78	Trevor Brooking	-
1978–79	Alan Devonshire	Bryan Robson
1979–80	Alvin Martin	Ray Stewart
1980–81	Phil Parkes	Geoff Pike
1981–82	Alvin Martin	-
1982–83	Alvin Martin	Phil Parkes
1983–84	Trevor Brooking	Tony Cottee
1984–85	Paul Allen	Tony Cottee
1985–86	Tony Cottee	Frank McAvennie
1986-87	Billy Bonds	Mark Ward
1987–88	Stewart Robson	Billy Bonds
1988–89	Paul Ince	Julian Dicks
1989–90	Julian Dicks	Stuart Slater
1990–91	Ludek Miklosko	George Parris
1991–92	Julian Dicks	Steve Potts
1992–93	Steve Potts	Kevin Keene
1993–94	Trevor Morley	Matthew Holmes
1994–95	Steve Potts	Tony Cottee
1995–96	Julian Dicks	Iain Dowie
1996–97	Julian Dicks	Iain Dowie
1997–98	Rio Ferdinand	Steve Lomas
1998–99	Shaka Hislop	Ian Pearce
1999–2000	Paolo Di Canio	Trevor Sinclair
2000–01	Stuart Pearce	Paolo Di Canio
2001–02	Sebastien Schemmel	David James
2002–03	Joe Cole	Jermain Defoe
2003-04	Matthew Etherington	Michael Carrick
2004-05	Teddy Sheringham	Mark Noble
2005-06	Danny Gabbidon	Marlon Harewood

A TOP 10 FINISH

A look back at the 2005–06 Premiership

NOT since that marvellous 1985–86 season when the Hammers attained a final finish of third place in the top Division have West Ham United fans enjoyed themselves as much as last year.

Having earned promotion back to the Barclays Premiership through the Play-Off final victory over Preston North End, after two years out of the top flight, the critics forecast that it would be a fight for survival and tipped the Hammers as one of the favourites to go straight back down.

But having bought shrewdly in the summer transfer market Pards, who had earmarked his defence as the area that needed strengthening the most, achieved that. He made four influential signings who added quality and flair to the squad making it a more competitive all-round unit with greater strength in depth.

The defence was bolstered by the arrival of Danny Gabbidon, Paul Konchesky and James Collins, while in midfield a wisp of a lad from Israel, Yossi Benayoun, proved to be a giant in midfield embroidering his delicate skills into the Premiership challenge.

It was imperative to get off to a good start and the 3-1 demolition of visiting Blackburn Rovers was achieved in style after a shaky first-half during which the visitors held the upper hand. But after the break it was a different story and once Teddy Sheringham had opened the account with the Hammers first goal of the season to make it 1-1 the tide turned.

What a difference a goal makes. Suddenly the players believed in themselves and no longer intimidated went about dismantling the Rovers' defence taking the lead with a truly special goal. Nigel Reo-Coker crowning a marauding charge forward with a bullet of a shot that left goalkeeper Friedel for dead. Matty Etherington added a third.

A goalless draw at Newcastle followed to help boost confidence even further and the run continued with just two defeats suffered in the opening 10 League and Cup games.

Two of the highlights from this run were the 4-0 eclipse of Aston Villa under the Upton Park floodlights and a 0-0 draw with mighty Arsenal.

The Villa game was a big night for Marlon Harewood who not only scored his first ever Premiership goal but went on to claim his first hat-trick since joining the Club from Nottingham Forest in November 2003.

It was not just the fact that the Hammers had scored four goals that was so uplifting as the quality of the play. This was sheer entertainment, a game good enough to remind us that this is the beautiful game when played in the right spirit with ambition and flair.

Teddy Sheringham, as ever, was the creative spark around which West Ham's attacks revolved. His instinctive vision and delicate flicks and touches complimented by the busy legs of Marlon Harewood, Bobby Zamora, Nigel Reo-Coker and Yossi Benayoun would be the catalyst for the season.

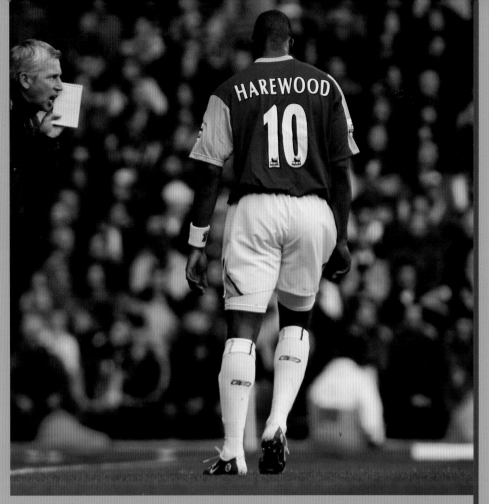

The arrival of Arsenal at Upton Park was always going to be a severe test and one that the Hammers passed with flying colours. There were no goals but this was English football at its traditional best and by the close of play it was the Hammers dressing room that was more disappointed that they had not got the victory they perhaps deserved.

There was a similar feeling at White Hart Lane where Anton Ferdinand had snatched a point out of defeat with an equalising headed goal deep into stoppage time.

The Hammers did not deserve to be a goal down as the fourth official flashed up the time added on by the referee and when a corner was forced everyone piled forward including goalkeeper Shaka Hislop.

Paul Konchesky delivered the corner from the right with his cultured left-foot, curling the ball across the face of the Tottenham goal towards the far post.

Big Shaka, resplendent in a vivid yellow jumper, was hardly inconspicuous as he launched himself forward. Thankfully, he missed the ball allowing Anton to take

advantage and steer his header down and past England goalkeeper Paul Robinson.

The home fixture with Manchester United is always one of the treats of a season and on an emotional night following the death of George Best it was Marlon Harewood who seized the initiative blasting in an unstoppable shot inside the opening minute.

United clawed back a 2-1 win, however, with goals from Rooney and O'Shea to which the Hammers responded in the very best way with a 2-1 victory at Birmingham City.

Bobby Zamora and Marlon Harewood were the winning scorers, Zamora's goal an exhibition of sublime skill and technique that left one open mouthed with admiration.

December was not a particularly profitable month in terms of results but the win at St Andrews and the 2-1 triumph at Goodison Park, where Bobby Zamora was on target again, were uplifting enough in terms of making nonsense of the Hammers reputation of uncertainty when playing away.

Although losing rather unfortunately 3-2 at Blackburn, the harvest of six points from three

successive away games emphasised what at that time was the most exhilarating spell of the season and after 17 games West Ham United was ninth in the Premier table – just one point behind Arsenal.

The New Year opened in defeat, at home to the Champions Chelsea, but a measure of the team had been their resolve and ability to bounce back from such disappointments and they responded magnificently reeling out seven consecutive victories in League and Cup.

A 2-1 away victory over Aston Villa was very pleasing for the team had under-performed in the first-half and trailed by a goal. However, they raised their game in the second-half to clinch a thoroughly deserved win with Marlon Harewood destroying the Midlands giants for the second time this season when he notched his fourth goal in two games against them.

Bobby Zamora had headed the Hammers level from a pin-point free-kick off the boot of Paul Konchesky and Marlon converted a penalty to clinch the points after Delaney had handled Hayden Mullins' goal-bound shot.

If this was good then the best was yet to follow for on Wednesday, February 1st, the Hammers chalked up a landmark victory, and probably the best of the season in the Premiership, beating Arsenal 3-2 at Highbury.

The Gunners were taken out by two absolutely fantastic goals. The first from Nigel Reo-Coker who beat Sol Campbell in a challenge then streaked away down the centre of the pitch towards the Arsenal goal. This was a difficult one for young Nigel for when through one-on-one with the goalkeeper you are expected to finish. On the other hand he had so much time to think about it he might well have been caught in two minds.

But no such failings here for the young skipper as he strode on to coolly slide his shot under German international goalkeeper Jens Lehmann.

Hardly had the fans had time to draw breath than Bobby Zamora left Campbell floundering

before executing the sweetest of finishes as he curled a left-footed shot into the far corner.

Arsenal were in disarray although Henry deflected a Pires shot past Shaka Hislop to give them hope. However, even though Pires claimed a goal himself late on Matthew Etherington had already taken advantage of a hesitant defence to hit a third goal for the Hammers 10 minutes from time.

It was in this game that the Club's new record signing, England Under-21 international striker Dean Ashton, made his debut replacing Bobby Zamora for the final 16 minutes.

The winning sequence was ended at Bolton where there was no score in the Fifth Round of the FA Cup and back in the Premiership Sam Allardyce's team then secured an emphatic 4-1 win against a make-shift Hammers side when Pards opted to rest players in order to keep them sharp for the Cup battles ahead.

Indeed, the latter part of the season was dominated by the Cup although victories over Manchester City, West Bromwich Albion and Tottenham Hotspur were enough to secure a final ninth place finish.

And what better way to conclude a Premiership season than with a rousing 2-1 home win over Tottenham Hotspur.

The Tottenham team had been hit by sudden sickness and food poisoning was suspected after a pasta meal at the team's hotel. But this was later ruled out as the source of their inconvenience which was attributed to a virus within the squad.

Whatever, their pleas to have the game replayed were never going to be upheld and the two stunning goals from Welsh international Carl Fletcher, now with Crystal Palace, and Israeli international Yossi Benayoun were good enough to sink any team.

REMEMBER

HAMMERS OFFICIAL ANNUAL 2007

The Hammers contested their fifth FA Cup final when they took on Liverpool at the Millennium Stadium last May and were only seconds away from victory in one of the greatest finals of modern time.

ROUND 3: NORWICH CITY (0) 1 WEST HAM UNITED (1) 2

Pards told the players, "a good season can become a great one if you reach the final or even win it. Why not?" Hayden Mullins opened the campaign within six minutes at Carrow Road when accepting Zamora's pass he hit the net with a crisp shot from 18 yards. Bobby made victory certain with a fearless diving header to take advantage of an error by England goalkeeper Robert Green. City clawed one back from the penalty-spot but the outcome was never in doubt.

ROUND 4: WEST HAM UNITED (2) 4 BLACKBURN ROVERS (1) 2

Rovers scored within 27 seconds and for half-an-hour looked comfortable. Then Khizanishvili, under pressure from Bobby Zamora, handled in the box and Teddy, shaping as if to blast his penalty, cheekily chipped it straight down the middle with the goalkeeper plunging to his right. Four minutes later, Yossi's tenacity and Zamora's clever side-steps set up Matty Etherington who picked his spot. Shaka made a couple of fine saves to deny Mokoena before the unfortunate Khizanishvili turned Konchesky's driven cross into his own net, 3-1. Rovers hit back and at 3-2 the floodlights failed. But Bobby Zamora shone again pouncing on Friedel's parry to net his first home goal of the season.

ROUND 5: BOLTON WANDERERS (0) 0   WEST HAM UNITED (0) 0

It was end to end at the Reebok but even though Marlon Harewood, Bobby Zamora and Teddy Sheringham were all used during the course of the game the impasse remained and it finished goalless.

ROUND 5 R: WEST HAM UNITED (1) 2 BOLTON WANDERERS (1) 1 *aet

Marlon Harewood lashed in the winner in the 95th minute after Etherington and Benayoun had paved the way for a cross to the near post. It climaxed an exciting night at Upton Park. Hunt's own-goal off Marlon's driven cross had given the Hammers a 10th minute advantage. Then Davies levelled the scores in the 31st minute. No further goals until extra-time when Matty showed great control sold the perfect dummy to slip Yossi in. His low cross to the near post was met by Marlon who crashed the winner in.

ROUND 6: MANCHESTER CITY (0) 1   WEST HAM UNITED (1) 2

On a cold night at the City of Manchester Stadium, Dean Ashton warmed Hammers hearts with a two goal flourish. The defining moment in a hard fought tussle came in the 41st minute. 'Deano,' cut in from the left, exchanged passes with Marlon, Matty and Nigel, then held off a challenge. Working the ball from his right to his left he opened up a gap through which he dispatched a stunning left-foot thunderbolt that beat David James on his near post. With a semi-final place the prize the competition became fierce but with Christian Dailly crumpled in agony by the touch-line, Nigel and Yossi, unaware of their injured colleague's plight, played on. Yossi clipped his cross beyond James' grasp for 'Deano' to deliver the *coup de grace* from close range. Musampa volleyed an 85th minute reply but the hammer blows had been struck.

SEMI-FINAL AT VILLA PARK: MIDDLESBROUGH (0) 0   WEST HAM UNITED (0) 1

Semi-finals are always tense and it was agonising for 78 minutes. Then Ashton instinctively flicked the ball to Harewood who used his strength to hold off Southgate's challenge and rifle an unstoppable rising shot into the roof of the net. It was far from over as Boro put an increasingly frantic Hammers defence under intense pressure. In the fifth minute of stoppage-time the ball fell to Riggott, totally unmarked six yards from goal, it seemed all could be lost. But the Boro defender thrashed his shot wide. West Ham were in the Cup Final.

FINAL AT THE MILLENNIUM STADIUM: LIVERPOOL (1) 3 WEST HAM UNITED (2) 3 *aet

Liverpool won 3-1 on penalties.

It was acclaimed as one of the great finals of modern time. The Hammers were just four minutes stoppage-time away from FA Cup glory – leading Liverpool 3-2 in a real thriller – when Steven Gerrard launched a right-foot missile that almost broke the net and took the tie into extra-time. West Ham had taken the lead in the 21st minute, when Carragher deflected Lionel Scaloni's low driven cross into his own net. 1-0 became 2-0 seven minutes later when goalkeeper Reina spilled the ball and Ashton pounced to tuck it in. Cisse pulled one back with a super close-range volley. Just after the break Reina made a crucial double save from Matthew Etherington and then Yossi Benayoun and the pendulum swung Liverpool's way in the 54th minute when from Crouch's knockdown Gerrard made it 2-2 from 12 yards. But the young Hammers, far from deflated, regained the lead when Paul Konchesky's cross sailed over the keeper's head. Alas, the bubble was burst by Gerrard's thunderbolt finish. A goalless extra 30 minutes in which West Ham went closest to scoring when Reina tipped Nigel Reo-Coker's goal-bound header against a post was followed by the lottery of a penalty shoot-out that went Liverpool's way 3-1... but there was honour in this defeat after such a fantastic final!

STRIKE

The Hammers scored 52 goals in the first season back in the Barclays Premiership and a further 18 goals in FA Cup and Carling Cup- ties – 70 goals in all spearheaded by a strike force that blends the subtlety and creativity of Teddy Sheringham with the power and pace of Marlon Harewood, the heading strength of Dean Ashton and the guile and enthusiasm of Bobby Zamora. This is a strike force to be reckoned with as Premiership defenders have realised to their cost.

MARLON HAREWOOD

The piano-playing, hip-hop DJ, strikes the right note when it comes to scoring goals as for the third successive season he finished as the Hammers leading goal scorer.

Hotshot Harewood, who was born and raised in Camden, North London, is a powerfully built athlete who can frustrate at times when not making the best use of his physical attributes but when in full flight his power and his pace can be a match for anyone.

The manager has frequently deployed him on the right side of a five man midfield with the brief to exploit his speed and burn the turf to support the front man.

"I like to stay in the middle because I want to score as many goals as possible for the team. That's how I see my job as a striker," says Marlon. "But whatever the gaffer wants I don't like to say no.

"What I do know is that when I play there I occupy centre-halves when I get the ball."

In a pre-match interview before the vital FA Cup semi-final with Middlesbrough, Marlon suggested: "When you get this far in the Cup, you have to seize the moment."

Profound words and he lived up to his own advice when in the 78th minute having taken Dean Ashton's pass in his stride he held off the challenge of Boro skipper Gareth Southgate to blitz an unstoppable rising shot into the roof of the net – one chance, one goal, Marlon had shot the Hammers into the Final!

Goals are his business and he claimed 17 of them last season and none came quicker in the whole of the Barclays Premiership than Marlon's thunderbolt that put the Hammers into the lead in the home game with Manchester United. It was struck in just 52 seconds.

Dubbed 'The BFG' (Big Friendly Giant) by skipper Nigel Reo-Coker, Marlon will refer to his first goal against Aston Villa as one of his favourites. Put through by the elegant Teddy Sheringham he coolly slid his shot under the advancing goalkeeper. It was really special for Marlon as it was his very first goal in the Premiership.

It became even more significant as Marlon added a second and then a third goal to register his first ever hat-trick for West Ham United.

Marlon's Most Important Goal

There were so many good goals to reflect on but his winner in the FA Cup semi-final against Middlesbrough at Villa Park was the most significant.

FORCE

TEDDY SHERINGHAM

At the age of 40, most players are entering the next stage of their life but for Teddy Sheringham this is still to come as he continues playing at the highest domestic level, obviously not as much as he used to because Alan Pardew naturally rests him when he can.

Although the former England, Manchester United and Tottenham Hotspur star might well have contemplated ending his career at the very top following last season's FA Cup Final appearance Pards – the 20th manager under whom Teddy has played - was anxious to persuade him to continue for another season.

The legs inevitably become weary but Teddy was never ever graced with pace. His success and fame at both international and club levels have been achieved through a natural quality that is purely instinctive and impossible to coach into players.

He has the knack for being in the right place at the right time, a sort of sixth sense, and when talking of him reading the game like a book – well, Teddy is simply a chapter ahead of most of his opponents.

The truth is he still has a special gift and it is not just the subtlety of his touch, the elegance of his movement, both on and off the ball, or the calmness of his finishing. It is his overall influence on everyone around him.

Teddy is the ultimate professional, a dedicated athlete who has looked after his body and is the perfect role model for all young players to emulate.

Yet he claims: "I'm not teaching them at all. I'm still learning the game as well. If I see Bobby Zamora do something great, I'll think 'how did he do that?' You never stand still in this game."

Teddy is the oldest player currently competing in the Barclays Premiership but insists: "I'm still hungry. I want to play football. I don't want to sit and watch."

Teddy's Most Important Goal

Teddy scored the winning goals in the home games against Middlesbrough and West Bromwich Albion and was our only success in the penalty shoot-out in the FA Cup Final. But the most crucial was the one that made it 1-1 at home to Blackburn on the opening day of the season and inspired a 3-1 victory for a perfect Premiership start.

DEAN ASHTON

'Deano' became the Hammers most expensive player when Norwich City received £7.25 million for his registration in January and the England Under-21 international, who made his debut from the substitute's bench in the latter part of the Hammers 3-2 win at Highbury on February 1, showed his worth with some important goals.

Dean is not blessed with blistering pace but he is physically strong, very competitive, and besides holding the ball up well makes many chances for his colleagues with some very perceptive off the ball running that pulls defenders away and creates space.

Alan Pardew believes that Dean can become "an old-fashioned number 9" and not surprisingly his style of play has drawn comparisons with Alan Shearer.

Only twelve months after enduring the heartbreak of relegation in the Norwich City side that was demoted in the final game of the season at Fulham Dean fulfilled a life-time ambition by scoring in an FA Cup Final.

It was a great piece of opportunism, pouncing on the ball that had been spilled by Liverpool goalkeeper Reina to make it 2-0.

He says: "No one can ever take that away from me now that I have played and scored in an FA Cup Final. But you know for a couple of weeks it did not matter to me anyway because we didn't win.

"It is not the best feeling in the world to lose such an important game like that obviously. What can you say? Four minutes to go your only thoughts are you are going to win and lift the Cup. So for Gerrard to score with that amount of time left was devastating. Credit to him, there is not many players in the world who could produce that.

"I don't think we could have done any more. Obviously you can look back at chances we had to seal the game. But to score three goals in an FA Cup Final against Liverpool – to do much more than that is asking a hell of a lot and everyone was absolutely shattered in the dressing room afterwards. No one could have given any more."

Dean's Most Important Goal

His first against Manchester City in the FA Cup quarter-final at Eastlands.

BOBBY ZAMORA

Another local lad from Barking, Bobby achieved a life-long ambition when he joined the Hammers from Tottenham Hotspur in a part-exchange deal that took Jermain Defoe to White Hart Lane in February 2004.

Already a film star after releasing a DVD diary of the Hammers Play-Off triumph over Preston in 2005, in which he scored the goal that earned promotion to the Barclays Premiership, the former England Under-21 striker was the hero again with a wonder goal at Birmingham City last season that thrilled an even bigger audience as it was shown live on Sky Sports.

With his back to goal Bobby received the ball from Marlon Harewood and as he was closed down from behind he flicked the ball over the City defender, spun, side-stepped centre-back Upson, then showing incredible tight control and balance waltzed around a desperate lunging challenge from Johnson. Regaining his balance he shot through goalkeeper Vaesen's legs from the tightest of angles.

This was the goal as Bobby saw it: "I flicked the ball over the full-back's head and sort of danced past a couple and because it was so tight the only place I could see was through the goalkeeper's legs. So I just tried to stick it there."

If he had been a Brazilian stiker no doubt that goal would have been repeatedly shown on television for evermore, nonetheless it emphasised that a lad from Barking could emulate the technique of the masters.

Bobby can be electrifyingly exciting as he was in the FA Cup victory over Blackburn Rovers when after the floodlights went out he lit up Upton Park with the final clinching goal.

A passionate West Ham United fan from his early days in the East End he always plays with zest and enthusiasm for the Club he loves.

He says: "There is an excellent spirit in the squad and qualifying for Europe was one of our ultimate aims last season. We achieved that and now we have to aim even higher. There's no point standing still."

Bobby's Most Important Goal

His winner against Preston in the Play-Off Final that clinched the Club's return back to the Premiership. But for sheer magic that strike at St Andrews has to be a winner and it was also his 90th League goal in a career that has taken him from Bristol Rovers via Brighton & Hove Albion and Tottenham Hotspur to West Ham United.

WORD SEARCH

Figure out what words the clues represent. Then find the words in the grid. Words can go horizontally, vertically and diagonally in all eight directions. Answers on page 61.

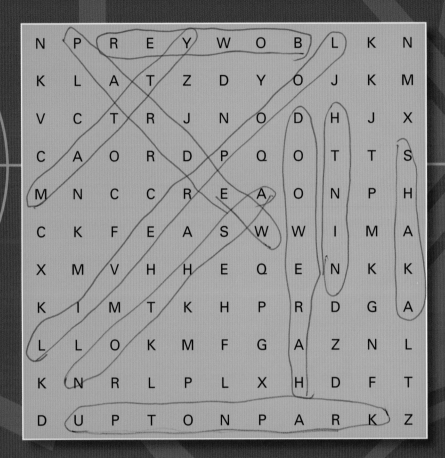

N	P	R	E	Y	W	O	B	L	K	N
K	L	A	T	Z	D	Y	O	J	K	M
V	C	T	R	J	N	O	D	H	J	X
C	A	O	R	D	P	Q	O	T	T	S
M	N	C	C	R	E	A	O	N	P	H
C	K	F	E	A	S	W	W	I	M	A
X	M	V	H	H	E	Q	E	N	K	K
K	I	M	T	K	H	P	R	D	G	A
L	L	O	K	M	F	G	A	Z	N	L
K	N	R	L	P	L	X	H	D	F	T
D	U	P	T	O	N	P	A	R	K	Z

Club record signing

Return to Hammers from Newcastle

Last season's leading scorer

Cup Final opponents

.... Etherington

Final Premiership position last season

Present boss

New senior coach Keith

Former goalkeeper

Hammers play here

HAMMERS'
YOUNG LIONS

FOLLOWING England's dismissal from the World Cup in Germany it was all change at FA headquarters with former Middlesbrough boss Steve McClaren taking over the managerial responsibilities from Sven Goran Eriksson and David Beckham handing in his captain's armband.

All eyes are now focussed on the European Championships, the finals of which will be staged in the summer of 2008, and with the team badly needing a transfusion of new blood West Ham United's starlets are very much in the frame.

Dean Ashton, who scored twice last season for the England Under-21 side, and left-sided pair Paul Konchesky and Matthew Etherington will all be in the running as surely will be several other young Hammers.

Skipper NIGEL REO-COKER was on Sven's stand-by list for the World Cup Finals in Germany but had to drop out because of injury. Nonetheless, his very inclusion as a stand-by for the most

prestigious football tournament in the world was acknowledgement of just how highly the young Hammers' skipper is rated at international level.

Nigel was outstanding captaining the England Under-21 side directing operations from midfield. Unfortunately, he was ruled out of the two vital Play-Off games with France to determine who would qualify for the European Under-21 Championship finals last summer, due to a serious ankle injury that kept him out for six weeks.

The team floundered to defeat over the two-legs without his considerable influence but Nigel is expected to be one of the key figures in McClaren's future plans.

Last season was a momentous one for the elegant play-maker whose compact physique makes him hard to shrug off the ball. His industry and determination matches his unbridled skills making him an all-round midfielder. Nigel has a bite in his tackle, an eye for the telling pass and a capacity for running that puts him in the Duracell class.

A youngster, who speaks eloquently about the game, he is a natural leader and became the youngest captain in the Nationwide First Division when handed the armband by Wimbledon boss Stuart Murdoch at just 19. A responsibility he now holds at Upton Park after Pards made him the Hammers' youngest ever skipper.

Indeed, Nigel captained West Ham United in the FA Cup final against Liverpool last May just one day short of his 22nd birthday, but the party was spoiled by that penalty shoot-out finish. Still, as a passionate deep-sea fisherman he has made many a big catch and is determined to reel in a few more big fish from the Premiership this season.

This might only be the second season of competitive football at Premiership level for ANTON FERDINAND, but last season he was far from overawed by his step-up to the top division and proved his ability against the best strikers the Premiership has to offer.

Following in the footsteps of his elder brother Rio, Nigel has graduated from the Hammers Academy to establish himself as a regular for both club and country, participating last season at centre-back in every game the England Under-21 side played.

Anton, who is said to have impressed Barcelona, was nominated for the PFA Young Player of the Year award after a wonderful season was topped by an outstanding performance in the FA Cup Final. It was his 100th senior appearance for the Club and such a pity it ended in tears when he became the third West Ham player to miss from the spot in the nerve-racking shoot-out climax that left Liverpool the victors.

Anton did not deserve such agony, but he could put it down to experience that he can draw upon as his career develops further as it surely will. For 'Jar Jar Binks', as some of the lads call him after the character in Star Wars, is a great all-round defender with the potential to go all the way at club and international levels.

Striker CARLTON COLE, signed from Chelsea in the summer, might not have been wanted by Jose Mourinho who gave him only nine

Premiership games last season and two in the Champions League having farmed him out on loan to Wolverhampton Wanderers, Charlton Athletic and Aston Villa in previous seasons, nevertheless the young hopeful has demonstrated his class when starring for the England Under-21 side.

"Goal-king Cole" was the headline after Carlton had scored three times in two young-England games impressing coach Peter Taylor enough to have him suggest he was destined to become an England regular.

Taylor claimed: "I think he has the potential to go all the way to play for the England first-team on a regular basis in the future."

Carlton is a very difficult opponent for defenders to contain. He is strong, works very hard and climbs impressively in the air and is very quick over the ground for a man of six-foot-three.

Both Tottenham Hotspur and Celtic were after his signature last summer but the 22-year-old saw Upton Park as his best opportunity of making the grade with England.

You can understand why Hammers' fans will be looking forward to the European Championships next year with ever greater interest with the prospect of our Young Lions playing their part as England roar to a long awaited success in a major international competition.

SUMMER SIGNINGS

As the Hammers prepared for their second season back in the FA Barclays Premiership, and a return to European action, manager Alan Pardew went on a summer recruiting mission to strengthen the squad.

JONATHAN SPECTOR

Born in Chicago, Jonathan was a regular in the USA Under-17 team when he was snapped up by Manchester United in November 2003 and impressed when taking the senior stage as a substitute for John O'Shea in United's 3-1 defeat by Arsenal in the Community Shield match at the Millennium Stadium in August 2004. He was in the starting line up at left-back for the 1-1 Premiership draw at Blackburn Rovers later that month and gained Champions' League experience with appearances against Dinamo Bucharest and Fenerbache.

Jonathan also made the first of his full international appearances for the USA as a substitute in a World Cup qualifying tie with Jamaica, but the arrival at Old Trafford of Gabriel Heinze pushed him down the United pecking order and he spent last season on loan with Charlton Athletic where he dislocated a shoulder and ruled himself out of any chance of making the USA World Cup Finals squad.

Essentially a left-back he is comfortable in any position right across the back line.

TYRONE MEARS

A right-back who is unbelievably fast and strong in the tackle, Tyrone made one substitute appearance in Manchester City's First Division Championship winning season of 2001-02 in a 3-0 home win over Nottingham Forest in March 2002.

Four months later he was snapped up by Preston North End, who paid £175,000 for his transfer, but his time at Deepdale was spoiled by injuries – a stress fracture of the shin, which was to keep him out for 14-months, being the worst of them. During his spell of action he had showed his versatility when used as a central-defender against the Hammers at Upton Park excelling at a man marking job on David Connolly.

Last season he changed his name in the hope it would bring him better luck and 'Tye' completed an injury free pre-season for the first time in four years.

LEE BOWYER

The first big-name signing of last summer the feisty midfield terrier returned to Upton Park having left the Club for Newcastle United following the team's relegation from the Premiership in 2003.

Brought in by Glenn Roeder to add bite to a struggling West Ham side, Lee played with the handicap of a damaged ankle during that first period at Upton Park and was unable to produce his best form.

A graduate from the trainee ranks at Charlton Athletic he was still a teenager when Leeds United paid £2.6 million for his registration in the summer of 1996 and he went on to feature in 203 Premiership games for them, scoring 38 goals, before the cash strapped Yorkshire club had to offload and he joined West Ham United in January 2003 for £100,000.

Capped once by England, Lee was in superb form for Newcastle United in the latter part of last season and brought with him a wealth of experience at domestic and European levels.

CARLTON COLE

A graduate from the Chelsea Academy, Carlton first came to prominence in the 2001-02 season when he scored 37 goals for the youth and reserve teams at Stamford Bridge and was named Chelsea Young Player of the Year.

He was given his senior debut in April 2002 with an entry from the substitute's bench in Chelsea's 3-0 home win over Everton and started in the final two games of that season scoring on his first full start with a header in a 2-0 win at Middlesbrough.

Carlton also scored at Charlton on the opening day of the following campaign, but although honoured with selection for the England under-21 side (which he later captained), he soon found himself in the shadows of the expensive foreign imports at Stamford Bridge and went on loan to Wolves.

He returned to the Bridge later that season and scored winning goals in consecutive games at Sunderland and home to Bolton Wanderers. But unable to secure a regular game with the 'Blues' he gained most experience on loan at Charlton Athletic and Aston Villa.

Reaching the FA Cup final last season earned the Hammers the bonus of a place in the UEFA Cup this season no matter the result as Liverpool had already qualified for the Champions League. It was a welcome back to European competition where West Ham United have a proud and distinguished record.

WEMBLEY STADIUM, May 19, 1965 and West Ham United surprised the world with a virtuoso performance against the German side TSV Munich 1860 in the final of the European Cup-Winners' Cup.

Alan Sealey was the two goal hero, but on a night when English football made its mark the whole team was magnificent. It was the first time an English side had out-passed and outplayed a Continental side and the 2-0 victory could have been even more emphatic had John Sissons not seen two tremendous efforts hit both the post and bar.

As it was Alan Sealey's two hits were good enough. His first goal, struck from the tightest of angles, his second snapped up after TSV failed to properly clear a Bobby Moore free-kick, was just the icing on the European cake.

The Hammers European adventure started after beating Preston North End in the 1964 Final of the FA Cup thus qualifying to represent England in the European Cup-Winners' Cup.

It started very modestly with a 1-0 victory in Belgium. Ronnie Boyce's goal against La Gantoise produced a result that overshadowed a moderate performance. Nonetheless, as the Belgian Cup winners' forced a 1-1 draw at Upton Park in the second-leg Ronnie's goal proved decisive.

It was another close-call in the Second Round with Sparta Prague. Johnny Sisson's goal in Prague edging a 3-2 aggregate victory that set up a Third Round meeting with Lausanne.

Brian Dear and Johnny Byrne secured a 2-1 win in Switzerland but any thoughts of an easy passage in the return-leg at Upton Park were quickly dispelled when Kerkhoffs headed the Swiss in front to make it 2-2. It triggered a seven-goal thriller which only swung the Hammers way in the final minute when Brian Dear smashed in his second goal of the game to make it a 4-3 victory on the night.

Dear opened the scoring against Real Zaragoza in the semi-final and Byrne volleyed in a spectacular shot from 18-yards to make it 2-0. But the Spanish hit back and it was down to another away goal from Johnny Sissons to clinch a 3-2 aggregate victory over the Spanish side and that date with TSV Munich 1860 at Wembley.

In 1966 The Hammers went out to Borussia Dortmund by a 5-2 aggregate at the semi-final stage but a decade later were back in the final of the ECWC having overcome opponents from Finland, the USSR, Holland and West Germany to earn the right to play Anderlecht.

In the Heysel Stadium, Billy Bonds set up the opening goal with a cushioned header for Pat Holland to stroke past goalkeeper Ruiter. But the Belgians equalised when a back-pass from Frank Lampard (Senior) held in the long grass. Van der Elst – who later became a Hammer – gave Anderlecht the lead and although Keith Robson made it 2-2, with a header that went in off a post, Anderlecht regained the advantage from a Rensenbrink penalty and went on to win 4-2 when Van der Elst claimed his second goal of the game.

A fourth appearance in the Cup-Winners' Cup (1980-81) was terminated by Dynamo Tbilisi in the Third Round and it was 19 years before Upton Park was able to enjoy the thrills of European competition again in the Intertoto Cup.

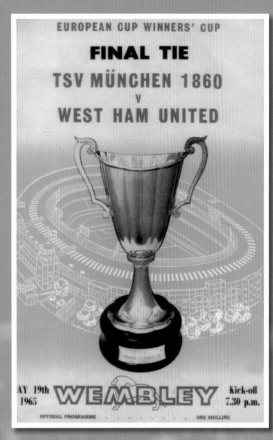

Having eliminated the Finns from Jokerit, and the Dutch side Heerenveen, a 3-2 aggregate victory was dug out against French side Metz after losing the first-leg of the final 1-0 at Upton Park. Sinclair and Lampard (Junior) shot West Ham into the lead and although Metz levelled on aggregate Wanchope pounced to seal victory.

This triumph qualified West Ham to compete in the UEFA Cup which got off to a great start with NK Osijek (Croatia) comprehensively beaten 6-1 on aggregate in the First Round.

Unfortunately, for the first time in Europe the Hammers were unable to score a single goal over two-legs in the Second Round with Steaua Bucharest. Joe Cole, Paolo Di Canio, Paulo Wanchope and Paul Kitson missed chances or were denied by goalkeeper Ritli in a goalless second-leg at Upton Park and the Romanian's took the tie 2-0 on aggregate.

Alan Pardew will be aiming to go a lot further this season and you never know, the Hammers could again become Kings of Europe.

FAMOUS FANS

KING OLAV OF NORWAY

A keen follower of football and a great admirer of the way the Hammers play he enjoyed his trip to Upton Park on November 12, 1988, when Nottingham Forest were the visitors in what turned out to be a Royal thriller.

JOHN CLEESE

Don't mention the score! But the king of silly walks and the inspiration behind comedy classics such as Monty Python and The Life of Brian was on his feet celebrating with everyone else when Frank Lampard Senior scored the goal that beat Everton in the FA Cup semi-final replay at Elland Road in April 1980.

GRAHAM GOOCH OBE

The famous England and Essex cricketer who became the most prolific run-scorer top class cricket has ever seen taking the lead from Jack Hobbs with 44,841 first-class runs and 21,087 in one-day games, has always been a West Ham United fan and has formed many friendships with the players.

Currently the official Ambassador for Essex County Cricket Club, he is not so involved now but while an active cricketer himself he often worked on his own fitness by joining the lads in training at Chadwell Heath.

PHILL JUPITUS

Another comic who loves the Hammers, the star of the TV show Never Mind The Buzzcocks is a regular at Upton Park. He was once a cartoonist on the West Ham fanzine Fortune's Always Hiding.

DAVID ESSEX

The Pop idol has followed West Ham United since 1956 when he and his friends packed into the old "Chicken Run." The music man, who has been at the top of his trade for four decades, tells us how "Bubbles" became the Hammers anthem. He says: "There was a big advert around in the 1930's for Pears Soap, which featured a kid with curly hair named 'Bubbles.' One of the West Ham schoolboy players looked just like him, so the nickname stuck and the supporters sang the song whenever he appeared on the pitch. That tune has been a trademark for Hammers fans ever since.

RAY WINSTONE

The film star who has appeared in classic films such as Scum and Sexy Beast and played Henry VIII in the Shakespeare masterpiece, is a Hammers fanatic and a regular in the Dr Martens Stand.

Other famous personalities who support the Hammers include, former boxing Champion Frank Bruno and TV presenter and former athlete Kriss Akabusi.

KRISS AKABUSI

FRANK BRUNO

QUIZ TIME!

Here are a few teasers to test your knowledge on the Hammers and the game of football generally. Why not take on your Dad and see who comes out on top? Three points for every right answer which can be found on page 60-61. Best of luck.

HAMMERS LEGENDS

1) Who holds the record for the most League goals scored? Is it Johnny Byrne, Vic Watson, Geoff Hurst or Tony Cottee?

2) Who commanded the highest transfer fee when leaving Upton Park? Was it Rio Ferdinand, Frank Lampard, Joe Cole or Bobby Moore?

3) Who holds the distinction of most appearances for the Hammers? Is it Bobby Moore, Trevor Brooking, Billy Bonds or Martin Peters?

4) Who scored the Hammers first ever FA Cup final goal at Wembley? Was it Jimmy Greaves, Geoff Hurst, Jimmy Ruffell of John Sissons?

5) Who was the most expensive goalkeeper to play for West Ham United? Was it Phil Parkes, Ted Hufton, Ernie Gregory, Noel Dwyer or Mervyn Day?

6) Who is he? He was a Hammers defender of some repute in the 1950s and went on to manage Crystal Palace, Manchester City, Plymouth Argyle, FC Sporting Lisbon, Middlesbrough and Bristol Rovers as well as coaching the Kuwait national team. Is it John Bond, Dave Sexton, Frank O'Farrell or Malcolm Allison?

7) This fellow headed the winning goal against Arsenal in the 1980 FA Cup Final. Who is he?

8) He made a scoring debut at home to Tottenham Hotspur on New Year's Day 1983 and went on to score 145 goals in 335 appearances for the Hammers before joining Everton. Who is he?

9) There has been no greater hot-shot from the spot than this Scot. He scored 76 of the 86 penalties he took. Was he Neil Orr, Frank McAvennie, Ray Stewart or Bobby Ferguson?

10) How many England caps did Bobby Moore win? Was it 98, 100, 108 or 110?

THE WORLD CUP

The finals were played only last summer but how much of the Greatest Show on Earth do you remember?

1)   In which country were the 2006 World Cup Finals staged?

2)   Who was the former Hammers' striker who scored the first goals that Germany conceded?

3)   Who was the Hammers' goalkeeper who played against England

4)   Name the former Hammers' striker who scored for the Ukraine against Saudi Arabia

5)   What was the result in the England v Ecuador match?

6)   Name the former Hammer who scored for England in the 2-2 draw with Sweden

7)   Who knocked Brazil out of the tournament? Was it Italy, Argentina, Portugal or France?

8)   Who knocked England out?

9)   Who were the four semi-finalists?

10) Who scored the winning penalty for Italy in the Final shootout with France?

WORD GAME

Re-arrange these jumbled letters to reveal the names of six West Ham United stars

1)   EASREMWLKJA (two words 5 & 6)

2)   RHCNOCHSEI (5 & 5)

3)   MTARDHYNEIHGEDS (5 & 10)

4)   NORDNADTNFIAEN (5 & 9)

5)   NADOMOLERHWAOR (6 & 8)

6)   SANOIYBNUOEYS (5 & 8)

These days of multi-million stars it's all a matter of science, as Niall Clark, Head of Hammers' Technical Support Team, explains...

YOU know it is not that long ago that footballers training was based on laps around the pitch and scaling the terraces up and down, up and down. And before the game the staple pre-match meal was steak, tea, toast and honey.

Such preparation for a professional football outfit is laughed upon now as the game has developed into a scientific exercise with practically every muscle movement monitored and analysed; every morsel that is devoured recorded.

One of the major signings manager Alan Pardew made following promotion to the Premiership was that of Niall Clark who was appointed Head of Technical Support.

What does that mean? "Well, basically I am the Sport Scientist which means I am responsible for all the day-to-day training of the players on a physiological basis. That means monitoring and maintaining their fitness levels," said Niall.

The game is faster, the play more intense, and with bodies almost at maximum stretch for 90 minutes or more the strain on the muscles is enormous leaving them far more vulnerable to pulls and strains.

Prevention is always better than the cure and Niall and his department, which consists of himself, three physiotherapists, two masseurs and a fitness coach, focus prominently on preventative measures.

A players' body is all important and Niall has free reign to determine on issues such as the intensity of the training on a given day.

He explains: "It is important to work closely with the manager and we sit down together every morning before training to discuss intensity levels and what we each hope to achieve from the session – what the actual training schedule is, when we eat and so on."

Fitness is all important, of course, and possibly more so at a club like West Ham where the manager has a small squad from which to draw his 11 players. This is a winning business and it is imperative that he should have his strongest players to call upon.

Says Niall: "I obviously can't prevent contact injuries or training ground incidents such as that to Roy Carroll last year when he injured his knee in a freak accident having got his foot tangled up with a goal net. But we can keep pulls and strains down to a minimum."

Niall and his team have done remarkably well in this respect while, of course, another crucial

aspect of their work is in the rehabilitation of injured players.

Recovering from muscle pulls and tears can be a lottery at times. There is always the danger that an enthusiastic player desperate to get back as soon as possible will push himself too hard and further damage the injury effecting an even longer absence from the team.

To have a knowledgeable, reliable instructor to bounce one's intentions off is not only comforting but re-assuring for the injured party.

As soon as an injury has been diagnosed a programme of rehabilitation is planned out probably involving weights' sessions to help rebuild the muscle, intense physiotherapy work and sessions with Niall who works closely with the physios (Steve Allen and Paul Hunter) all the time to see how the injured players are progressing.

Niall, 35, graduated from Brunel University with a Masters in Sports Science and was the head of PE at a London school before working with Alan Pardew at Reading Football Club where he served for five years.

Obviously pleased to see that the scientific approach has taken off in English football he says we have been lagging someway behind Europe in this respect.

Since its inception, Sports Science has revolutionised the game of football in England claims Niall who points out: "Alan is a very bright manager and if he didn't find it useful he wouldn't use it.

"It really does work and I can't emphasise enough how important a role it plays in today's football."

WING WIZARD MATTY

IT'S a sight to excite. The spectacle of a wide man tearing down the flank dropping a shoulder as if to weave inside then exploding down the outside to leave the wrong-footed defender in his wake as he delivers the final cross.

Goals are made and scored by such passages of movement. The delivery of the cross is all important and it can be the lifeblood for the waiting pack of strikers.

Wingers used to be two-a-penny, every club fielded two, usually one tricky dribbler and one more direct fast man. But the modern game has evolved in other directions preferring to flood the midfield and the winger's role is now more often than not filled by a midfield player moving wide and by the liberal use of wing-backs.

Yet there can be no substitution for a natural winger, a line-hugging player who has poise and balance; who naturally runs with the ball and has the skill to take people on and the technique to deliver the pin-point cross.

The dearth of such magicians was clearly seen in last summer's World Cup Finals in Germany. Sven Goran Eriksson utilised former Hammer Joe Cole on the left flank of the England attack. Yet talented as young Joe is he is never a natural winger his instinct favouring to cut inside rather than go wide and spread the play.

The truth is these days wingers are hard to find, but the Hammers are blessed with such a talent in the form of Matthew Etherington.

Matthew hails from Truro in Cornwall and is a very quiet reserved individual off the field, but once the whistle blows he sheds his cloak of secrecy and becomes a rampaging terror capable of destroying the best organised defences in the Premiership.

There are none who appreciate his contribution more than Dean Ashton, Marlon Harewood, Bobby Zamora and Carlton Cole who thrive on his crosses.

Last season, manager Alan Pardew led a host of admirers imploring Sven Goran Eriksson to include Matty in his World Cup plans, a voice that was backed by Hammers World Cup winning legend, Martin Peters, who felt he would be the perfect answer to England's left-sided problems.

Enthused Martin: "Matty can go past people and has a great left foot. I think he would do well at that level."

Matthew, by his own admission, took a little while to come to terms with readjusting to life in the Premiership and reflected: "The tempo is much higher than it was in the Championship and obviously it was a massive step-up. But I think we have thrived on that you know. We do play better on the big occasions as we showed in the Cup Final against Liverpool."

Wingers are valuable assets to any team, great wingers are priceless, and Matt obviously, at the age of 25, is still improving his game and raising his ambitions to make his mark in one of the toughest domestic competitions in world football.

BACK AT THE TOP

THERE are not many full-backs who can boast having scored in an FA Cup final, but Paul Konchesky enjoyed such a moment of glory when in the 63rd minute at the Millennium Stadium his perfectly delivered cross beat Liverpool goalkeeper Jose Reina all ends up to fizz into the top corner.

Alas, the joy of giving the Hammers a 3-2 lead was to end in tears as the heartbroken defender submitted to his emotions after missing in the penalty shoot-out that was to steal victory from under our noses and take the trophy to Anfield.

The opportunity to spend June and July in Germany also eluded Paul when he just missed out on selection for the England World Cup squad after making his second full international appearance in the friendly win over Argentina in Geneva.

"It was a flick of a coin between me and Wayne Bridge," says Paul who has been capped by England at every level from the age of 15. Nonetheless, he will be a serious contender for the national side for the European Championships.

His fresh youthful looks can be disarming, especially for those opponents who try to take him on, for Paul Konchesky is quick, strong, fearsome in the tackle and following a great initial season at Upton Park seems set to become the Hammers' best left-back since Julian Dicks.

Paul has the same insatiable appetite and spirit for the game as had the former cult-hero and has already endeared himself to the supporters who appreciate his competitive edge and determination. This should be no surprise for him as born in Barking, he was an avid West Ham fan and grew up with Bobby Zamora, Jermain Defoe, John Terry and Ledley King.

They are all from this manor, and all have graduated from Sunday morning football on Wanstead Flats - where Terry, King and Paul were formidable defenders behind Bobby Zamora playing for a team called Senrab FC in the Echo League Premier Division. Terry, Defoe, King and Paul have since gone on to play for the full England team.

As a kid Paul would knock on the door at the nearby house of Paul Ince and ask him to come out for a kick about in the local park. Incey had not long become a national figure after scoring twice against Liverpool in a League Cup-tie at Upton Park.

"He never came out – his Mum always said that he wasn't there," reflects Paul who adds: "As I grew, I became a big fan of Julian Dicks, who gave everything for West Ham. And I couldn't get enough videos on Paolo Maldini, the best left-back in the world, and the fact he is right-footed says an awful lot about what he achieved."

Paul played for the Hammers as a boy, but at the age of 14 drifted south of the Thames to secure a foothold in the game with Charlton Athletic where, in August 1997, he became their youngest ever debutant when, at the age of 16-years and 93-days, he started at left-back in a 3-2 home win over Oxford United.

During his eight years at The Valley, Paul enjoyed some wonderful times and finished just one short of 150 League appearances but 58 of those were from the bench and many featured him in a midfield role.

KONCH FACTFILE

Born: Barking, Essex, May 15, 1981

Height: 5ft 10ins

A trainee with Charlton Athletic he signed professional in May 1998

Played for Tottenham Hotspur on loan September – December 2003

Joined West Ham United: July 5, 2005 (£1.3 million)

Hammers Debut: Blackburn Rovers (h) FA Barclays Premiership August 13, 2005

International: England (2) v Australia & Argentina

In the summer of 2003 he asked to go on the transfer list because he wanted to play left-back, his favoured position, but when Tottenham Hotspur took him on loan to have a look at him they also utilised his services in a midfield role.

Back at The Valley the consensus of opinion continued to suggest that midfield could well be Paul's best position. However, remaining un-persuaded he continued to believe in himself as a left sided wing-back and when Alan Pardew sought his services for that very position offering him the opportunity to join the team of his dreams he had no hesitation in leaving The Valley for Upton Park in the summer of 2005.

Paul convincingly proved his case in a season in which he excelled and there is no doubt he has the tools and commitment to follow 'Dixie' into the book of West Ham United legends given time.

The lad from Barking links up well with 'Matty' Etherington on the left flank and is an important supply line for Marlon, Teddy, Dean and Bobby at the sharp end. As he says: "My job is to create goals and stop the goals as well." And, of course, occasionally grab one for himself as he did in the Cup Final.

WHO AM I?

A

Can you identify this West Ham United defender from these 10 clues?

Clue 1: I am six-feet tall

Clue 2: I am 25-years old

Clue 3: My playing position is left-back

Clue 4: I was born in Belfast

Clue 5: I was a trainee with Sunderland

Clue 6: I won a Coca-Cola League Championship winners' medal

Clue 7: I captained my previous club

Clue 8: I moved to West Ham last August

Clue 9: I made my Premiership debut when I was 19-years-old

Clue 10 I have played international football for Northern Ireland at Schoolboy, Youth, U-21 and full levels

B

Can you puzzle out who this West Ham United striker is?

Clue 1: I am a local lad from Barking

Clue 2: I have always supported West Ham since a kid

Clue 3: I used to come to matches as a schoolboy along with Paul Konchesky and John Terry

Clue 4: My sporting hero is Tony Cottee

Clue 5: I have a Staffordshire bull terrier called Zeus

Clue 6: I also have a huge DVD collection

Clue 7: The lads call me "Peanut Head"

Clue 8: My first club was Bristol Rovers

Clue 9: I turned down the chance to play for Trinidad & Tobago as West Ham were more important to me at the time.

Clue10: I scored the goal that beat Preston at the Millennium Stadium

C

Who is this motivator from the engine room?

Clue 1: I was brought up in Southwark, South London

Clue 2: I was a young Don

Clue 3: I supported Liverpool as a kid

Clue 4: I am a gadget freak

Clue 5: I love to annoy Teddy with my music in the dressing room

Clue 6: The first car I ever bought was a sky blue Fiat Punto

Clue 7: I scored my first goal for West Ham against Wimbledon

Clue 8: I religiously watch Eastenders on TV

Clue 9: Steven Gerrard is the best player I have ever played against

Clue10: I scored five goals last season

The answers can be found on page 60–61

DID YOU KNOW?

MARK NOBLE

1. He hails from Newham
2. He became the youngest player ever to play for the Reserves when aged 15
3. He won the Young Hammer of the Year award in 2005
4. He made his full Premiership bow at Tottenham Hotspur in November 2005
5. He captained the England Under-18 international team
6. He made his Hammers debut as a 17-year old against Southend United in the Carling Cup (August 2004)
7. He played for Hull City on loan last season but was injured and had to return to Upton Park
8. His hero and inspiration as a schoolboy was Joe Cole
9. He is nicknamed 'Hollywood' by the lads as he always likes to do the spectacular
10. He is strong in the tackle, fearless in the challenge

KYLE REID

1. He was born in South London
2. His 19th birthday is November 26, 2006
3. He joined the Hammers in July 2004
4. He is 5ft 10ins tall
5. He has represented England at youth levels from Under-16 upwards
6. He is a fast running left winger
7. He made his senior bow in the starting line at West Brom in the Premiership last May
8. He was given the opportunity when Matty Etherington felt his hamstring tighten in the warm-up
9. He can also play on the right wing
10. He scored five goals for the Hammers in the FA Premier Academy League Under-18s last season

EDWARD (Teddy) SHERINGHAM

1. He was born in Highams Park and was a Hammers fan as a kid
2. He served his football apprenticeship with Millwall
3. He remains the Lions most prolific scorer having claimed 93 League goals in their colours
4. He was transferred to Nottingham Forest for £2 million in July 1991
5. He returned to London a year later for the first of two spells with Tottenham Hotspur
6. He next became a Manchester United hero in their treble winning season 98-99 winning the Premiership title, FA Cup and Champions League
7. He came off the bench in the Champions League Final to score the equalising goal against Bayern Munich and set-up the stoppage-time winner
8. He had a season with Portsmouth before joining the Hammers on a free in July 2004
9. He starred for England in Euro 96 and scored 11 goals in 51 England appearances.
10. He finished his first season at Upton Park as Hammer of the Year

JOHN PANTSIL

1. He was born in Ghana
2. He started his career playing for Berekum Arsenal FC
3. He was in the Ghanaian international team that reached the final of the FIFA World Youth Championships in 2001
4. He joined Maccabi Tel Aviv in 2002
5. He won an Israeli championship winners' medal in 2003
6. He transferred to Hapoel Tel Aviv in 2004
7. He represented Ghana in the African Cup of Nations finals in 2002 (Mali) & 2006 (Egypt)
8. He played in all four of Ghana's games in the World Cup Finals in Germany
9. He joined West Ham United in August 2006
10. He is 25 and plays fullback or as a holding midfield player

SUPER SAVERS

ROY CARROLL, who joined the Hammers on a Bosman free transfer from Manchester United in the summer of 2005, missed out on all the thrills and excitement following surgery on a troublesome back injury that limited him to just 19 appearances last season.

The Northern Ireland international, who was a trainee with Hull City and played for Wigan Athletic before joining the Old Trafford staff, is a highly competent shot stopper and was so unlucky to miss out on the opportunity of making his third FA Cup final appearance in consecutive years.

Roy had starred at the Millennium Stadium for Manchester United in each of the two previous finals earning a winner's medal against Millwall and a runners-up trophy the following year when having been outplayed by Manchester United for the majority of the game the Gunners hammered out a victory in a penalty shoot-out.

At 29 Roy still has years ahead of him and he has been so impressed with the youngsters in front of him he believes that Pards has the makings of one of the best Hammers teams ever.

JAMES WALKER – fulfilled a life-time ambition when he made his Premiership debut in the Hammers home game with Portsmouth last March.

The popular goalie, who always wears a smile on his face no matter what, had spent 11 years with Walsall – where in his early days he had to take his kit home to wash it himself – before signing for West Ham United in June 2004.

Although kept on the fringe he never lost heart and towards the latter part of the 2004–05 season found himself holding the fort and playing against Preston North End in the Play-Off final.

Unfortunately, having helped win promotion to the Premiership James was unable to enjoy the fruits of his endeavours until the following March after sustaining cruciate ligament damage in the 87th minute of that final in Cardiff.

ROBERT GREEN – became Alan Pardew's seventh signing of the summer when he agreed a deal with Norwich City.

Robert graduated from the junior ranks at Carrow Road to keep a clean sheet on his League debut for the Canaries in a goalless draw in the big East Anglia derby with Ipswich Town in 1998-99. But it was not until the campaign of 2001-02 that he was established as City's number one.

Born in Chertsey, Robert overcame a serious back injury as a youngster to become the cornerstone of the Canaries' excellent defence that went on to clinch the First Division championship in style in 2004 and he was outstanding in his first season in the Premiership.

A laid-back unflappable character Robert had been capped by England at all youth levels and was rewarded with his first full international selection when he played in the second-half against Colombia in New York in May 2005.

Set to travel to Germany last summer as one of England's three World Cup goalkeepers he unfortunately suffered a serious groin injury and had to withdraw.

Now fully fit Robert has a great future as the Hammers number one goalkeeper.

SUPER SKIPPERS

BOBBY MOORE OBE (1958–73) who is the most famous Hammer of them all, captained West Ham United to FA Cup victory in 1964 and a year later lifted the European Cup Winners' Cup. But his crowning glory, of course, came in 1966 when he led England to victory in the World Cup Final against West Germany at Wembley.

He wasn't particularly fast or good in the air but none read the game better than Bobby who was strong in the tackle and possessed an uncanny knack of snuffing out danger before it threatened. The timing of his interceptions was perfect and at his peak Bobby was the greatest defender in world football winning total respect from the likes of Pele.

Bobby played 108 times for England, 90 of them as captain (which was a world record shared with Billy Wright), yet when he was first picked for a friendly international against Peru in 1962, Bobby became the first West Ham United player to win automatic selection for England since Len Goulden who won 14 caps between 1937 and 1939.

An elegant athlete, Bobby wasn't an arm raised battle cry captain but led by example communicating his instructions and support to his colleagues in a non-pretentious manner. He tragically died of colon cancer in February 1993 when only 51.

ALVIN MARTIN (1978–96) was an elegant footballing centre-half whose stature and demeanour just commanded respect. A Liverpudlian developed through the Hammers' junior ranks he has never lost his Scouser sense of humour. He took over the key centre-half role from Tommy Taylor in 1997-98 and won the first of his 17 England caps when he was 22, and played in the World Cup Finals in Mexico in 1986.

Alvin was in the 1980 FA Cup winning team and won a runners-up medal in the League Cup final. He took over the captaincy from 'Bonzo' in 1984 and led the Hammers to that third place finish in 1985-86 the highest in the Club's history.

That season he too scored a hat-trick in an 8-1 win over Newcastle United at Upton Park, the unusual aspect being that he scored against three different goalkeepers.

BILLY BONDS MBE (1967–88) was the typical Boy's Own hero, a swashbuckling player who tackled hard and contested every ball and demanded equal commitment from those around him. Billy, during the time he sported long hair and a bearded chin, was every inch the ferocious warrior who led his men into battle. A dedicated professional signed from Charlton Athletic as a ball winning wing-half for £50,000 in May 1967 to add grit to the side he was probably the best buy manager Ron Greenwood ever made.

Appointed club captain in 1974, Billy was an inspirational leader going in where angels fear to tread, socks down around his ankles, arms bare, tackling with a ferocity that made him feared from Newcastle to Plymouth. And Billy was not just a destroyer he scored 59 goals including a hat-trick against Chelsea.

He twice captained West Ham to Cup Final successes against Fulham in 1975 and Arsenal in 1980 and he passed Bobby Moore's Club record appearances in the 1982-83 season going on to make 757 (12) appearances and playing his last game past the age of 40.

Billy was set to play alongside Alvin Martin for England against Brazil at Wembley but was denied his international cap by injury.

NOEL CANTWELL (1952–60) a big strong thick-set left back whose partnership with John Bond was probably the best ever at Upton Park. They, along with Malcolm Allison, were the tactical inspiration behind the promotion success of 1957-58.

Signed from Cork United in 1952, Noel made 248 League appearances for the Hammers stamping his authority on the team and opponents alike and he skippered the Hammers to the Second Division title in 1957-58. A strong willed man and a natural inspirational leader, he won 17 of his 36 caps for the Republic of Ireland while at West Ham and also played cricket for Ireland in 1956.

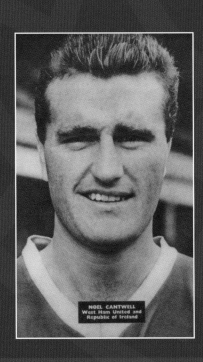

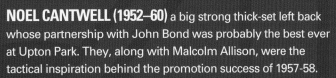

Noel became the most expensive full-back in football history when Manchester United paid £29,500 for him in November 1960 and three years later he collected the FA Cup as captain of the Red Devils.

He went on to become chairman of the PFA and finished his international career as player-manager of the Irish national team before concentrating on a career in management at club level with Coventry City and Peterborough United.

After retirement Noel became involved again on the international circuit as part of Sven Goran Eriksson's scouting network assessing future opposition. Sadly he passed away in hospital after a short illness on September 8, 2005 aged 73.

HAMMERS HISTORY

What do you know about West Ham United? Test your knowledge of your favourite club by tackling these 20 questions. Award yourself three points for every correct answer – one point if you are halfway there. Answers are on page 60–61.

1) Who was the Club's very first manager? Was it Ron Greenwood, Ted Fenton or Syd King?

2) What was the Club called before it became West Ham United in 1900?

3) The Club played in the Southern League or Essex League before their election to the Football League?

4) Hammers took up residence at the Boleyn Ground in 1904. Where did they play the home matches before that? Was it at Wanstead Flats, The Memorial Grounds or Newton Heath?

5) When Danny Shea was transferred to Blackburn Rovers in 1913 it was for a record fee. What was the figure? Was it £200; £2,000 or £20,000?

6) On August 30, 1919, The Hammers played their very first League game (in Division Two) at home and drew 1-1 against Liverpool, Leicester City, Lincoln City or Leeds City?

7) The first floodlight game played at Upton Park produced a 2-1 victory over Tottenham Hotspur. But what year was that? Was it 1933, 1943, 1953 or 1963?

8) West Ham United has played in five FA Cup Finals. True or false?

9) On April 28, 1923, West Ham United played in the very first FA Cup final to take place at the old Wembley Stadium. Who was it against and what was the final score?

10) In 1969 a famous area of the ground was demolished for development. Was it the East Stand, the West Stand or the Chicken Run?

11) Who scored the winning goal in the Hammers 3-2 FA Cup final victory over Preston in 1964? Was it Trevor Brooking, Ronnie Boyce, John Sissons or Geoff Hurst?

12) The Club paid a record fee for a goalkeeper when they signed Phil Parkes for £565,000 in February 1979. From which London club did big Phil come?

13) On December 3, 1988 the Hammers registered their 1,000th victory in the League with a 1-0 win at Millwall. Who scored the goal? Was it Paul Ince, Leroy Rosenior, David Kelly or Liam Brady?

14) Which German team did the Hammers beat at Wembley in the final of the European Cup-Winners' Cup in 1965?

15) Alan Pardew's first game in charge of West Ham United was on October 18, 2003. Hammers drew 2-2 against Burnley, Birmingham City or Blackburn Rovers?

16) Who was the manager who signed England goalkeeper David James from Aston Villa during the summer of 2001?

17) David James and Phil Parkes were England internationals. Can you name another Hammers goalkeeper who has played for England? Could it be Mervyn Day, or Ernie Gregory? Jim Standen or maybe Ted Hufton? The choice is yours.

18) What is the highest position West Ham United have finished in the League and what season was it achieved?

19) The Hammers reached the Play-Off finals in consecutive years 2004 and 2005, but who did they beat in the semi-finals?

20) Who holds the Club record for number of appearances? Is it Bobby Moore, Martin Peters, Geoff Hurst, Billy Bonds, Trevor Brooking or Alvin Martin?

Q 16

Q 14

How did you get on?

There was a maximum of 60 points available. If you got 50 or more then you really do know your Club history. 30–40 points is very, very good; 20–30 good. If you got less than that then try again.

Q 9

Q 1

IN THE NET!

For all the latest news, views and events from Upton Park, make sure you visit the Club's official website www.whufc.com

STAGE one of the website re-launch took place back in February, when the Club introduced a brand new design, new and exclusive player and editorial features, enhanced match coverage, plus a fantastic free Members Area that grants supporters access to a Pocket Pardew desktop character, exclusive downloads and a whufcmail. com email address.

Since then, whufc.com has consistently been named in the top six of most-visited Premiership club websites each month by the independent Comscore Analysis and, with over 350,000 unique users each month, 40,000 registered users on our database and almost 5million page impressions a month, the official website is rapidly growing.

Part two of our re-launch arrived for the beginning of the present Premiership campaign, including new and improved Junior Hammers and Vintage Claret sections, exciting new editorial features, and the introduction of WHUTV – our brand new premium broadband video service, giving supporters the opportunity to watch Premiership highlights every week, regular reserve and youth coverage, plus exclusive video interviews and behind the scenes footage with the players at our Chadwell Heath training ground.

Having taken such huge strides on the pitch since our return to the Premiership last year, West Ham United is working hard to continue our progress off the pitch. We see whufc.com as our main portal of contact between the Club and its supporters, and will also continue our policy of announcing all major player and transfer news on the website first as soon as it is confirmed.

Don't miss a moment of the action at Upton Park….visit www.whufc.com now!

GET INTO HAMMERS GEAR!

Solve all your present problems with a visit to the Club's Stadium and Lakeside Stores. All the latest kit and the very best in leisure wear for Hammers fans of all ages.

STADIUM STORE
Boleyn Ground, Green Street, Upton Park,
London E13 9AZ
Tel: 020 8548 2794

LAKESIDE STORE
Unit 71, Lakeside, Thurrock, Essex
Tel: 01708 890258

MAIL ORDER
Tel: 0845 4500098
Email mailorder@westhamunited.co.uk

ORDER ONLINE   whufc.com

OPEN TIMES   Monday–Friday 9.30am–5.00pm

Matchday opening times vary according to kick-off

A LONG DUSTY ROAD FOR YOSSI

YOSSI BENAYOUN was an instant hit with Hammers fans from the first moment he stepped onto the Upton Park pitch and displayed his delightful delicate skills.

Initial concerns that this slightly-built ball player might not be strong enough to hold his own in the robust physical world of English football were expressed. But only by those who did not fully appreciate the history of his coming to the big time.

Born into a family of Moroccan immigrants, Yossi knows exactly what it takes to survive. His parents struggled daily to raise their children in Dimona, a poor immigrant town in Israel's Negev Desert, where Yossi's flair for football was first recognised, as he kicked around on a dusty rutted pitch, by a scout from FC Hapoel Beer-Sheva.

Invited to join the club at the age of 10, he wasn't afforded the kind of assistance that youngsters in England would enjoy from their local club. For five years he and his father Dudu rose at dawn to hitch-hike the 30 kilometre route to Beer-Sheva.

Can you imagine playing for a team that is top of the Israeli League as a 15-year-old and having to make your way to the match by thumbing a lift? On the occasion of a top of the table clash with visiting second placed Maccabi Tel Aviv, he had been stuck for four hours in one place on Highway 54 unable to hitch a ride.

The game had started by the time Yossi got to the ground but 'The Kid' as he was known got on and scored a stunning hat-trick to sink the Tel Aviv club 3-1 and help clinch the Championship for FC Hapoel.

News in football travels fast and Yossi's rare talents were appreciated further afield, the Dutch giants Ajax no less inviting him to join them at their world renowned training centre in Amsterdam.

It was obviously an enormous step but to make him feel at home the Dutch club took his parents, his brother, sisters and his girlfriend to live with him in Holland.

Unfortunately, none of them settled and one by one the family, fuelled by homesickness, returned to Israel until finally only Yossi and his father were left. "Unhappy in his heart" Yossi was soon on a plane back to Israel himself.

His return was seen as failure by the Israeli press who branded him as being "too soft", but his career developed further following a transfer to Maccabi Haifa where he not only won two more Championships but was also honoured twice as the Israeli Player of the Year.

In 2002, Yossi felt mature and confident enough to accept the challenge of Europe again signing for Spanish club Racing Santander and his skills flourished not only in La Liga but for the Israel national side as well.

Yossi was excited when told of West Ham United's interest in him. He knew a lot about the Hammers having followed the fortunes of his hero and friend Eyal Berkovic who had been a crowd pleaser at Upton Park in 1997-98.

One telephone call to Eyal and Yossi was assured that the East End of London was the place for him although he admits that after making his debut against Blackburn Rovers on the opening day of last season he did have some doubts.

He explains: "Twenty minutes into the game I couldn't breathe. The pace of the game was different to anything I'd experienced before.

"Even the training was physically tougher to anything I had done before and it took some getting used to. But the lads were all very helpful and Teddy (Sheringham) told me to take it easy and build myself up slowly and I would get accustomed to the pace of the English game, and he was right.

"Teddy is a great guy to give you confidence and it is really exciting playing with great players like him."

Yossi has met the physical challenge head on and handled it well. But then such is what one expects from a lad who has fought his way from the hardships of poverty down the long dusty road that led him to an FA Cup final appearance and fame.

Teddy Sheringham

STAR-MAKER CARR

WE believe football is the greatest game in the world and that there is nothing that can give you more pleasure. Nonetheless, whether you are a top professional or a youngster starting out there is always room for improvement and at Upton Park the Hammers have probably the greatest star- maker in the country in Youth Academy Director Tony Carr.

Born in Bow on September 5, 1950, the son of an electrician with the London Electricity Board, Tony attended St Paul's Way School where he emerged as a talented, if not big, centre-forward and captained the East London Boys team, in which Pat Holland was a team-mate, to victory in the coveted English Schools Trophy in 1966.

It seemed then that he was destined for a career in football and on leaving school at 15, Tony was signed on by the Hammers as an apprentice impressing enough to be rewarded after three years with a full professional contract. Alas, two years later having played regular games in the reserves he was released.

It was a bitter blow and one that countless youngsters have suffered, but he didn't give up and eventually found fame in another direction.

After a short spell with Barnet, Tony unfortunately broke a leg and following complications had to give up all ideas of a professional career. After working as a PE instructor in local schools he was invited back to Upton Park by John Lyall to help coach the kids.

This has proved to be Tony's vocation for he has worked wonders over the past 25 years nurturing the skills of hundreds of youngsters.

It takes a special type of person to work with young players and Tony's record is without equal. Among the big names he has helped and honed into star material are Paul Allen, Tony Cottee, Paul Ince, Alan Dickens, Steve Potts, Kevin Keen, George Parris, Stuart Slater, Danny Williamson, Frank Lampard (Junior), Rio Ferdinand, Anton Ferdinand, Joe Cole, Michael Carrick, Glen Johnson, Chris Cohen, Elliott Ward, Mark Noble and Matthew Reed.

Tony works with potential professionals but the general principles for improving your game are the same at any level. Whether you just enjoy kicking around with your friends

or have deeper ambitions to make football a career the more you practice the better you will become.

You can work on improving your technique and lots of aspects of your game like touch and learning to kick the ball with your weaker foot. You can improve the way you strike a ball, your kicking, passing, heading and to a limited degree you can also increase your pace.

You can practice some of the basics on your own. Find a wall and kick the ball against it using alternative feet, right-foot, left-foot. Hit the ball hard against a wall and practice controlling the returning ball varying the height of delivery. A wall can also be useful to practice your heading against.

If you play for an organised team Tony has laid out a blueprint for making it better in a wonderful book entitled "How to Coach A Soccer Team."

This is aimed at coaches and people who run young teams giving advice on preparation, organisation, tactics and individual drills. Tell your coach about it. It could help you and your pals improve your game and become a winning team.

HAYDEN'S CUP FINAL DREAM

LAST season ended in glory for the Hammers even though they just missed out on the ultimate prize of lifting the FA Cup they had produced a performance to be proud of. However, for one man the emotions must have been almost unbearable.

Hayden Mullins, who had been one of the most consistent performers in the team all season, had to sit the Millennium thriller out having been suspended after being shown a red card in the home game with Liverpool.

Our hearts went out to the quietly spoken midfielder for although he performs in the business end of midfield it was so out of character for him to be involved in such a skirmish.

It seemed rough justice particularly as the former England Under-21 international had fired the opening shot that set the Hammers on their way to Cardiff. The goal he put past England goalkeeper Robert Green in the Third Round at Carrow Road had everyone jumping off their seats.

It seemed almost like slow-motion as Bobby Zamora wormed his way in from the Norwich City goal-line, leaving full-back Rossi Jarvis in his wake. Bobby then laid the perfect pass back towards Hayden who ran onto it and cracked a stunning shot that clipped the inside of the near post and fizzed into the back of the net. The Hammers one up in six minutes!

It was a real corker and Hayden's only goal of the season but having missed out on the big day he is now all the more determined to help drive the Hammers to a second successive Final appearance.

It all kicks-off again in the Third Round in January, and Hayden says: "The FA Cup is special. If you lose you are out for another year so if you go a goal down the emphasis is all on getting the goal back. So I think it is a different game to that in the Premiership and it makes for exciting watching and exciting playing and we all love the FA Cup.

"If you can get the right draw and the rub of the green then everything is possible. I don't think anyone could have foreseen us doing as well as we did last season reaching the Cup final and finishing ninth in the Premiership and qualifying for Europe.

"The Premiership is very competitive and you can't put in five-star performances every week. Although we are a good

footballing team it is not always possible to impress our game on the opposition for there are teams who will just sit back and absorb the play. We have found them difficult to break down.

"We are a team that likes to hit opponents on the counter attack and we did that to perfection at Arsenal and against Liverpool in the Cup final, because they came at us."

Hayden reached the quarter-finals of the FA Cup with his previous club Crystal Palace and the semi-final with the Hammers. Will 2007 be the year that he banishes the heartbreak of last May and fulfils his dream to play in the Final?

Anton Ferdinand

DID YOU KNOW?

10 things you might not know about…

JAMES COLLINS

1. He was born in Newport, Monmouthshire
2. He was 17 years-old when he made his senior debut for Cardiff City
3. His debut for the Bluebirds was in an FA Cup-tie against Bristol Rovers
4. He played for Wales against England in the World Cup qualifying tie in Cardiff
5. He made his Hammers debut against Everton at Goodison Park
6. He scored with a brilliant header at Chelsea but his first goal for the Hammers was at Portsmouth on Boxing Day
7. His nickname is 'Ginge'
8. He captained the Welsh Under-21 team against Germany in February 2005
9. His middle name is Michael
10. He became the first player to win caps at every level for his country when he made his senior debut for Wales against Norway in May 2004.

CHRISTIAN DAILLY

1. He was signed from Blackburn Rovers for £1.75 million in January 2001
2. His first club was Dundee United
3. He won a record 34 Under-21 caps for Scotland
4. He made his 500th club career appearance against Sunderland on Feb 4, 2006
5. He has captained the full Scotland team
6. He was transferred from Derby County to Blackburn Rovers for £5.3 million
7. He scored his first international goal for Scotland against Malta
8. He has been christened 'Braveheart' by Hammers skipper Nigel Reo-Coker
9. He has won Scottish and English FA Cup final medals with Dundee United and West Ham United
10. He scored against Ipswich to take the Hammers to the Play-Off final against Crystal Palace

SHAUN NEWTON

1. He hails from Camberwell in South London
2. He won a First Division Championship medal with Charlton in 2000
3. He scored 12 goals in 130 Premier/League games for Wolverhampton Wanderers
4. He created Wolves' first ever Premiership goal
5. He has been capped three times by England at Under-21 level (1996-97)
6. He made his Hammers debut at Reading on March 12, 2005
7. He scored with two headers for Charlton against Huddersfield Town – his second from 30 yards out!
8. He played for a Football League Under-21 side against an Italian Serie 'B' select team and scored in a 1-1 draw.
9. Up to the start of this season, though, he had only scored once for the Hammers. The winner against Manchester City on April 15, 2006
10. He is affectionately called 'Beetle' by the other lads

QUIZ TIME!

PREMIERSHIP TEASERS

How much do you know about the Hammers opponents in the FA Barclays Premiership? Test your knowledge with these posers. Answers are on page 60–61.

ARSENAL

The Gunners moved into their new Emirates Stadium at the beginning of this season, but where did they originally play? Was it at Plumstead Common, Clapham Common or Wimbledon Common?

ASTON VILLA

Name the England manager who also had two spells managing Villa? Was it Bobby Robson, Don Revie, Graham Taylor or Glenn Hoddle?

BLACKBURN ROVERS

Rovers have won the Premiership Championship once, in 1994-95. Was their manager Graeme Souness, Mark Hughes or Kenny Dalglish?

BOLTON WANDERERS

Who was the famous Bolton Wanderers centre-forward who after playing for England in Austria was hailed as 'The Lion of Vienna'? Was it 'Dixie' Dean, Nat Lofthouse, Tommy Lawton or Ted Drake?

CHARLTON ATHLETIC

Where did Charlton Athletic play their home games in 1991? Was it at The Valley, Selhurst Park or Upton Park?

CHELSEA

Can you name the former West Ham United forward who has managed Chelsea? Was it Sir Geoff Hurst, Len Goulden, David Cross or Jimmy Greaves?

EVERTON

The Hammers drew their Premiership game against Everton last season. Was the score 0-0, 1-1 or 2-2?

FULHAM

Who was the former French international who was in charge of Fulham before Chris Coleman? Was it Michel Platini, Gerard Houllier or Jean Tigana?

LIVERPOOL

Do you know who the Liverpool legend is who holds the club record for the most goals scored? Is it Kenny Dalglish, Ian Rush, Roger Hunt or Robbie Fowler?

MANCHESTER CITY

Manchester City was the only team to prevent the Champions Chelsea from scoring against them in the Premiership in 2004-05. Who was the former Hammers goalkeeper who shut the Blues out?

MANCHESTER UNITED

Who scored United's goal in their 1-0 victory over the Hammers at old Trafford last March? Was it Wayne Rooney, Ruud Van Nistelrooy or Ryan Giggs?

MIDDLESBROUGH

Gareth Southgate took over as the club manager last summer when Steve McClaren was appointed England coach. Southgate joined 'Boro from Aston Villa in 2001, but which London club did he previously play for? Was it Millwall, Crystal Palace, Fulham or Tottenham Hotspur?

NEWCASTLE UNITED

When Alvin Martin scored a hat-trick in the Hammers 8-1 victory over Newcastle United in April 1986 each goal was scored against a different goalkeeper. The third, a penalty, was put past an England striker who had gone in goal. Was it Alan Shearer, Malcolm Macdonald or Peter Beardsley?

PORTSMOUTH

Teddy Sheringham wore the blue shirt of Portsmouth in 32 Premiership games in 2003-04. How many goals did he score? Was it nine, 12 or 14?

READING

Steve Coppell took over as manager when Alan Pardew left the Royals to become the Hammers boss. For which famous club side did Coppell star as a winger?

SHEFFIELD UNITED

What do Martin Peters, Steve Bruce and Neill Warnock have in common?

TOTTENHAM HOTSPUR

A former Hammer holds the Tottenham Hotspur League scoring record with 220 goals. Is it Les Ferdinand, Clive Allen, Jimmy Greaves or Sergei Rebrov?

WATFORD

The Hammers very last game in the Coca-Cola Football League Championship was played at Vicarage Road where we won 2-1. Who scored his very first senior goal for the Hammers that afternoon? Was it Hayden Mullins, Rufus Brevett, Luke Chadwick or Anton Ferdinand?

WIGAN ATHLETIC

A current member of the Hammers squad holds the distinction of being Wigan Athletic's most capped player. Who is he?

ANSWERS

HAMMERS LEGENDS

1) Vic Watson 298 League goals (1920-35)
2) Rio Ferdinand £18 million to Leeds United
3) Billy Bonds 781/12 (1967-88)
4) Johnny Sissons v PNE (2-5-64)
5) Phil Parkes
6) Malcolm Allison
7) Trevor Brooking
8) Tony Cottee
9) Ray Stewart
10) 108

WORLD CUP

1) Germany
2) Paulo Wanchope who scored twice for Costa Rica in the opening game won by Germany 4-2
3) Shaka Hislop for Trinidad & Tobago
4) Sergei Rebrov
5) England 1 Ecuador 0 (Beckham)
6) Joe Cole
7) France
8) Portugal on penalties
9) Italy, Portugal, France & Germany
10) Fabio Grosso

WORD GAME

1) Jimmy Walker
2) Chris Cohen
3) Teddy Sheringham
4) Anton Ferdinand
5) Marlon Harewood
6) Yossi Benayoun

WHO AM I

A   George McCartney
B   Bobby Zamora
C   Nigel Reo-Coker

PREMIERSHIP QUIZ

Arsenal – Plumstead Common

Aston Villa – Graham Taylor

Blackburn Rovers – Kenny Dalglish

Bolton Wanderers – Nat Lofthouse

Charlton Athletic – Upton Park because The Valley had been closed down

Chelsea – Geoff Hurst (1979-81)

Everton – 2-2 (Marlon Harewood and Dean Ashton scored the goals)

Fulham – Jean Tigana

Liverpool – Former England World Cup winner Roger Hunt (245 goals 1959–69)

Manchester City – David James

Manchester United – Ruud Van Nistelrooy

Middlesbrough – Crystal Palace

Newcastle United – Peter Beardsley

Portsmouth –Teddy claimed nine Premiership goals that season

Reading – Coppell, capped 42 times by England, played for Manchester United

Sheffield United – Martin Peters, Steve Bruce and Neil Warnock have all been managers at Bramall Lane

Tottenham Hotspur – Jimmy Greaves (1961–70)

Watford – Anton Ferdinand in the 42nd minute

Wigan Athletic – Goalkeeper Roy Carroll who was capped nine times for Northern Ireland while at the JJB Stadium.

HAMMERS WORDSEARCH

N	P	R	E	Y	W	O	B	L	K	N
K	L	A	T	Z	D	Y	O	J	K	M
V	C	T	R	J	N	O	D	H	J	X
C	A	O	R	D	P	Q	O	T	T	S
M	N	C	C	R	E	A	O	N	P	H
C	K	F	E	A	S	W	W	I	M	A
X	M	V	H	H	E	Q	E	N	K	K
K	I	M	T	K	H	P	R	D	G	A
L	L	O	K	M	F	G	A	Z	N	L
K	N	R	L	P	L	X	H	D	F	T
D	U	P	T	O	N	P	A	R	K	Z

HAMMERS HISTORY QUIZ

1) Syd King

2) Thames Iron Works FC

3) The Southern League

4) The Memorial Grounds

5) £2,000

6) Lincoln City

7) April 1953

8) True

9) Bolton Wanderers won 2-0

10) The Chicken Run was dismantled to make way for the East Stand

11) Ronnie Boyce

12) Queens Park Rangers

13) They all played in that game but it was Paul Ince who accepted a gift goal when he was presented with a misdirected back-pass

14) TSV Munich 1860

15) Burnley

16) Glenn Roeder

17) Ted Hufton who won 6 England caps (1923–29)

18) Third in the old First Division in 1985–86 finishing behind Liverpool and Everton and eight points clear of Man United in fourth place

19) Ipswich Town winning 2-1 on aggregate in 2004 and 4-2 on aggregate in 2005

20) Billy Bonds 781/12 (1967–88)